CW01660783

MY NOTEBOOK OF MAGNETIC DREAMS & DESIRES

i am **divinely magnetic**
and trust that my glow
will **attract everything i need**
to make my dreams come true.
so i **daydream** in wonder
and dance with the **stars,**
and **let the universe** send me
the dreams of my heart.

MY DREAMS & DESIRES

/ /

TODAY I AM DREAMING OF:

buying a house by the sea

Use the spaces below to draw, write and explore your dream!

What can I see in this dream?

the turquoise sea
blue and white walls
flowers in the kitchen
my lush green sofa
the sunrise in the morning

What can I hear in this dream?

the seagulls outside
the sound of waves
music playing in the kitchen
the kettle boiling
my cat meowing

my bagel in the toaster
the salty sea air
fresh cotton bedsheets
my nag champa incense

What can I smell in this dream?

the warmth of the sun
my soft pyjamas
the sea breeze on my skin
my feet on the balcony

What can I feel in this dream?

HOW WILL I FEEL ONCE I HAVE RECEIVED & ACHIEVED THIS DREAM?

I will feel light, happy and content. I will feel safe, relaxed and secure.

I will feel in my flow state waking up by the sea each morning.

I will feel excited having my friends around for a BBQ in the garden!

HOW CAN I ALIGN AND ALLOW THIS DREAM?

IS THERE ANYTHING I NEED TO LET GO OF TO MAKE ROOM FOR THIS DREAM?

I need to let go of any preconceptions/ideas about how and where this house might show up and let the Universe surprise me!

DO I CURRENTLY NEED TO TAKE ACTION OR WAIT FOR THE NEXT STEP TO SHOW ITSELF TO ME?

I need to wait a few months until I have a deposit saved before I start house hunting again.

WHO DO I NEED TO BECOME TO RECEIVE THIS DREAM?

I need to become a person who is stable with their finances and committed to saving at least 20% of my wages each month.

ALIGNMENT PRACTISE > FEEL INTO YOUR DREAMS REALITY

MY CHOSEN SONG FOR THIS DREAM:

----

*Listen to this song and visualise/feel the reality of your dreams coming true on a daily basis - then, let the Universe show you the next step!

Choose one song that makes you feel the reality of your dream. For example, if you will feel excited, glowing and radiant when you receive your dream, choose a song that reflects this feeling.

PATHWAYS OF RECEIVING

LIST ALL THE WAYS THIS DREAM COULD HAPPEN:

- *I could buy a house by myself.*
- *I could buy a house with my partner or friend.*
- *I could be gifted some money in the next few months.*
- *I could be open to living in a different location.*
- *I could purchase a house with a shared ownership scheme.*
- *I could purchase a house with a low deposit scheme.*
- *I could increase my earnings and pay the deposit in full.*
- *I could receive support from my family.*
- *I could buy a house abroad and rent a home in my dream location*
- *I could sub-let a bedroom to support me to pay the mortgage.*
- *I could buy a house and rent it out in the summer months.*
- *I could live in a van whilst I save for my house.*
- *I could buy a cheaper house, renovate it and then sell it to make more money for buying my dream house.*
- *I could buy a plot of land and and build a house.*
- *I could move my savings into an account with more benefits.*
- *I could relax, chill out and just keep on saving.*

HOW CAN I STEP INTO LIVING THE VIBRATION OF THIS DREAM NOW?

Use the space on the following blank pages to explore how you can step into *living the vibration* of this dream now.

Book a few house viewings to boost my excitement!

Start spending more time & joining social activities in the area that I wish to live in!

Drive around different towns/ locations and notice which areas feel good to me.

Purchase small trinkets and paintings to display in my new home.

Visualise and listen to songs that make me feel as if I am already living in my dream house.

Visit furniture stores and get excited about how I plan to decorate my dream home.

SIGNS AND SYNCHRONICITIES

THESE INCLUDE:
SYMBOLS, ANGEL NUMBERS, SONGS, CONVERSATIONS, CHANCE MEETINGS, ETC.

DATE	SIGNS & SYNCHRONICITIES
/ /	Hearing my chosen manifestation song playing on the radio.
/ /	Seeing the angel numbers 555 and 888 everywhere!
/ /	Overhearing a conversation with useful information about shared ownership schemes.
/ /	Experiencing a chance meeting with someone who has a great deal of knowledge about buying land.
/ /	Receiving a surprise gift of money from a family member.
/ /	Seeing adverts for homes in my dream location everywhere.
/ /	Receiving signs and symbols in my dreams.
/ /	Being offered other opportunities in the area I am dreaming about buying my house in.
/ /	Receiving a call from the estate agents with a different, interesting offer.

CELEBRATING YOUR MANIFESTATION!

HOW DID I RECEIVE MY MANIFESTATION?

I received my dream through a pathway of connections!

Firstly, I kept overhearing conversations about a different town to the one I had been initially envisioning buying a house in.

Then, I began exploring other towns and felt drawn to a completely new area, so I started spending more time here.

A few weeks later, I received an unexpected call from the estate agents, saying that a beautiful house matching my requirements had dropped in price and was back on the market.

Finally, I received an unexpected gift of money which supported me to pay the deposit outright!

DID MY MANIFESTATION SURPRISE ME AT ALL?

Yes, initially I hadn't even considered living in the area in which I have now bought my home - it has blown me away!

Secondly, I didn't expect to purchase such a beautiful house at such a low cost.

Plus, I had no idea that I would be gifted a sum of money that would allow me to pay the full deposit!

THANK YOU UNIVERSE!

today i experience **miracle** after miracle -
today i experience more **magic**
than i could have ever imagined.

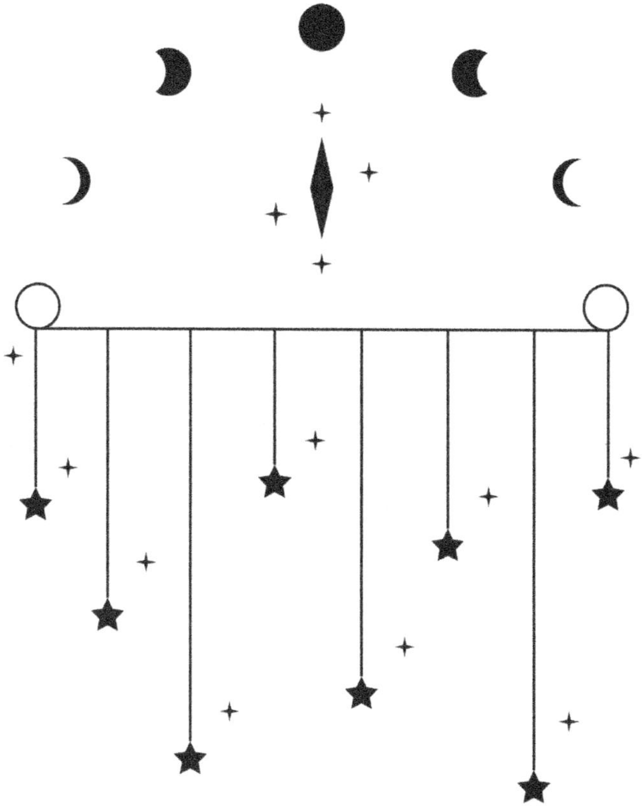

MY DREAMS & DESIRES

/ /

TODAY I AM DREAMING OF:

Use the spaces below to draw, write and explore your dream!

What can I see in this dream?

What can I hear in this dream?

What can I smell in this dream?

What can I feel in this dream?

HOW WILL I FEEL ONCE I HAVE RECEIVED & ACHIEVED THIS DREAM?

HOW CAN I ALIGN AND ALLOW THIS DREAM?

IS THERE ANYTHING I NEED TO LET GO OF TO MAKE ROOM FOR THIS DREAM?

DO I CURRENTLY NEED TO TAKE ACTION OR WAIT FOR THE NEXT STEP TO SHOW ITSELF TO ME?

WHO DO I NEED TO BECOME TO RECEIVE THIS DREAM?

MY CHOSEN SONG FOR THIS DREAM:

----

*Listen to this song and visualise/feel the reality of your dreams coming true on a daily basis - then, let the Universe show you the next step!

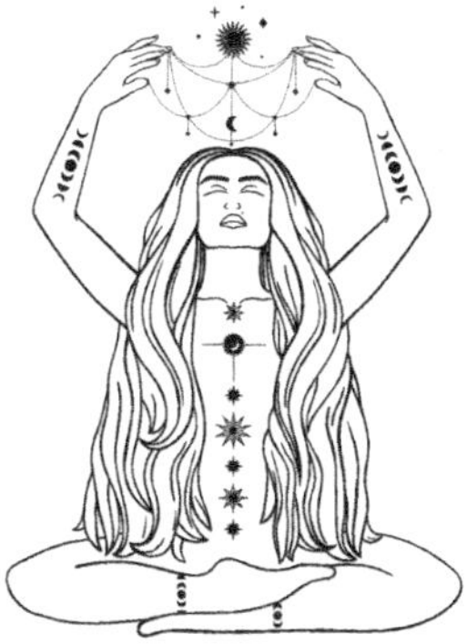

PATHWAYS OF RECEIVING

LIST ALL THE WAYS THIS DREAM COULD HAPPEN:

HOW CAN I STEP INTO LIVING THE VIBRATION OF THIS DREAM NOW?

Use this space to explore how you can step into *living the vibration* of this dream now.

SIGNS AND SYNCHRONICITIES

THESE INCLUDE:
SYMBOLS, ANGEL NUMBERS, SONGS, CONVERSATIONS, CHANCE MEETINGS, ETC.

DATE	SIGNS & SYNCHRONICITIES

CELEBRATING YOUR MANIFESTATION!

HOW DID I RECEIVE MY MANIFESTATION?

DID MY MANIFESTATION SURPRISE ME AT ALL?

THANK YOU UNIVERSE!

i am an **irresistible magnet**
for all that i desire,
everything i need
is created in the ether,
so i throw my heart to the sky
and **celebrate my vision**
as support floods in
and i **step into my mission.**

MY DREAMS & DESIRES

/ /

TODAY I AM DREAMING OF:

Use the spaces below to draw, write and explore your dream!

What can I see in this dream?

What can I hear in this dream?

What can I smell in this dream?

What can I feel in this dream?

HOW WILL I FEEL ONCE I HAVE RECEIVED & ACHIEVED THIS DREAM?

HOW CAN I ALIGN AND ALLOW THIS DREAM?

IS THERE ANYTHING I NEED TO LET GO OF TO MAKE ROOM FOR THIS DREAM?

DO I CURRENTLY NEED TO TAKE ACTION OR WAIT FOR THE NEXT STEP TO SHOW ITSELF TO ME?

WHO DO I NEED TO BECOME TO RECEIVE THIS DREAM?

MY CHOSEN SONG FOR THIS DREAM:

----

*Listen to this song and visualise/feel the reality of your dreams coming true on a daily basis - then, let the Universe show you the next step!

PATHWAYS OF RECEIVING

LIST ALL THE WAYS THIS DREAM COULD HAPPEN:

HOW CAN I STEP INTO LIVING THE VIBRATION OF THIS DREAM NOW?

Use this space to explore how you can step into *living the vibration* of this dream now.

SIGNS AND SYNCHRONICITIES

THESE INCLUDE:
SYMBOLS, ANGEL NUMBERS, SONGS, CONVERSATIONS, CHANCE MEETINGS, ETC.

DATE	SIGNS & SYNCHRONICITIES

CELEBRATING YOUR MANIFESTATION!

HOW DID I RECEIVE MY MANIFESTATION?

DID MY MANIFESTATION SURPRISE ME AT ALL?

THANK YOU UNIVERSE!

i am **whole in my being**
and centred in my worth,
gold dust surrounds me
as i speak **my magic word.**

____

MY DREAMS & DESIRES

/ /

TODAY I AM DREAMING OF:

_ _

Use the spaces below to draw, write and explore your dream!

What can I see in this dream?

What can I hear in this dream?

What can I smell in this dream?

What can I feel in this dream?

HOW WILL I FEEL ONCE I HAVE RECEIVED & ACHIEVED THIS DREAM?

HOW CAN I ALIGN AND ALLOW THIS DREAM?

IS THERE ANYTHING I NEED TO LET GO OF TO MAKE ROOM FOR THIS DREAM?

DO I CURRENTLY NEED TO TAKE ACTION OR WAIT FOR THE NEXT STEP TO SHOW ITSELF TO ME?

WHO DO I NEED TO BECOME TO RECEIVE THIS DREAM?

MY CHOSEN SONG FOR THIS DREAM:

----

*Listen to this song and visualise/feel the reality of your dreams coming true on a daily basis - then, let the Universe show you the next step!

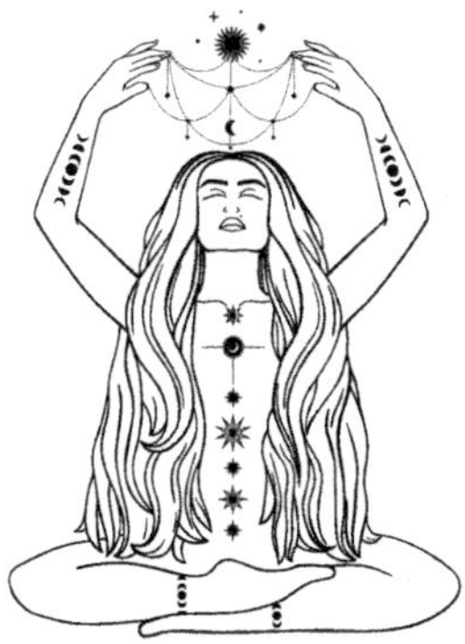

PATHWAYS OF RECEIVING

LIST ALL THE WAYS THIS DREAM COULD HAPPEN:

HOW CAN I STEP INTO LIVING THE VIBRATION OF THIS DREAM NOW?

Use this space to explore how you can step into *living the vibration* of this dream now.

SIGNS AND SYNCHRONICITIES

THESE INCLUDE:
SYMBOLS, ANGEL NUMBERS, SONGS, CONVERSATIONS, CHANCE MEETINGS, ETC.

DATE	SIGNS & SYNCHRONICITIES

CELEBRATING YOUR MANIFESTATION!

HOW DID I RECEIVE MY MANIFESTATION?

DID MY MANIFESTATION SURPRISE ME AT ALL?

THANK YOU UNIVERSE!

i ask with grace and allow with love
as i surrender to the divine design
of my highest living form -
as i live from alignment
things fall into place,
and i smile at the synchronicities
that guide me along the way.

MY DREAMS & DESIRES

/ /

TODAY I AM DREAMING OF:

Use the spaces below to draw, write and explore your dream!

What can I see in this dream?

What can I hear in this dream?

What can I smell in this dream?

What can I feel in this dream?

HOW WILL I FEEL ONCE I HAVE RECEIVED & ACHIEVED THIS DREAM?

HOW CAN I ALIGN AND ALLOW THIS DREAM?

IS THERE ANYTHING I NEED TO LET GO OF TO MAKE ROOM FOR THIS DREAM?

DO I CURRENTLY NEED TO TAKE ACTION OR WAIT FOR THE NEXT STEP TO SHOW ITSELF TO ME?

WHO DO I NEED TO BECOME TO RECEIVE THIS DREAM?

MY CHOSEN SONG FOR THIS DREAM:

----

*Listen to this song and visualise/feel the reality of your dreams coming true on a daily basis - then, let the Universe show you the next step!

PATHWAYS OF RECEIVING

LIST ALL THE WAYS THIS DREAM COULD HAPPEN:

HOW CAN I STEP INTO LIVING THE VIBRATION OF THIS DREAM NOW?

Use this space to explore how you can step into *living the vibration* of this dream now.

SIGNS AND SYNCHRONICITIES

THESE INCLUDE:
SYMBOLS, ANGEL NUMBERS, SONGS, CONVERSATIONS, CHANCE MEETINGS, ETC.

DATE	SIGNS & SYNCHRONICITIES

CELEBRATING YOUR MANIFESTATION!

HOW DID I RECEIVE MY MANIFESTATION?

DID MY MANIFESTATION SURPRISE ME AT ALL?

THANK YOU UNIVERSE!

i focus wisely and **choose to live divinely**
because my inner being knows,
that faith and hope and love and trust
will bring the winds that blow -
miracles into my life.

MY DREAMS & DESIRES

/ /

TODAY I AM DREAMING OF:

____

Use the spaces below to draw, write and explore your dream!

What can I see in this dream?

What can I hear in this dream?

What can I smell in this dream?

What can I feel in this dream?

HOW WILL I FEEL ONCE I HAVE RECEIVED & ACHIEVED THIS DREAM?

HOW CAN I ALIGN AND ALLOW THIS DREAM?

IS THERE ANYTHING I NEED TO LET GO OF TO MAKE ROOM FOR THIS DREAM?

DO I CURRENTLY NEED TO TAKE ACTION OR WAIT FOR THE NEXT STEP TO SHOW ITSELF TO ME?

WHO DO I NEED TO BECOME TO RECEIVE THIS DREAM?

MY CHOSEN SONG FOR THIS DREAM:

----

*Listen to this song and visualise/feel the reality of your dreams coming true on a daily basis - then, let the Universe show you the next step!

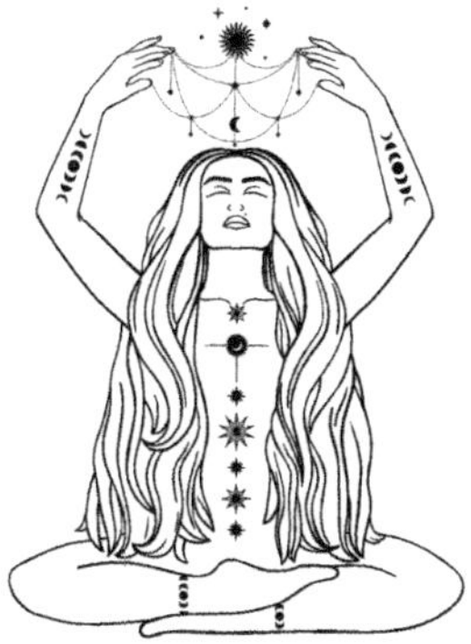

PATHWAYS OF RECEIVING

LIST ALL THE WAYS THIS DREAM COULD HAPPEN:

HOW CAN I STEP INTO LIVING THE VIBRATION OF THIS DREAM NOW?

Use this space to explore how you can step into *living the vibration* of this dream now.

SIGNS AND SYNCHRONICITIES

THESE INCLUDE:
SYMBOLS, ANGEL NUMBERS, SONGS, CONVERSATIONS, CHANCE MEETINGS, ETC.

DATE	SIGNS & SYNCHRONICITIES

CELEBRATING YOUR MANIFESTATION!

HOW DID I RECEIVE MY MANIFESTATION?

DID MY MANIFESTATION SURPRISE ME AT ALL?

THANK YOU UNIVERSE!

my dreams lay in a locket,
as **gold dust in my heart**
and when people ask me
'what are you daydreaming of love?'
i say quietly and kindly
'i'm keeping it close to my heart,
because i am birthing miracles
and **that is only just the start.'**

MY DREAMS & DESIRES

/ /

TODAY I AM DREAMING OF:

Use the spaces below to draw, write and explore your dream!

What can I see in this dream?

What can I hear in this dream?

What can I smell in this dream?

What can I feel in this dream?

HOW WILL I FEEL ONCE I HAVE RECEIVED & ACHIEVED THIS DREAM?

HOW CAN I ALIGN AND ALLOW THIS DREAM?

IS THERE ANYTHING I NEED TO LET GO OF TO MAKE ROOM FOR THIS DREAM?

DO I CURRENTLY NEED TO TAKE ACTION OR WAIT FOR THE NEXT STEP TO SHOW ITSELF TO ME?

WHO DO I NEED TO BECOME TO RECEIVE THIS DREAM?

MY CHOSEN SONG FOR THIS DREAM:

----

*Listen to this song and visualise/feel the reality of your dreams coming true on a daily basis - then, let the Universe show you the next step!

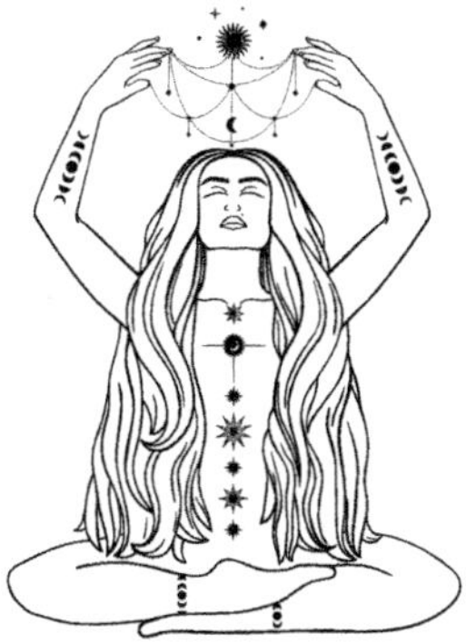

PATHWAYS OF RECEIVING

LIST ALL THE WAYS THIS DREAM COULD HAPPEN:

HOW CAN I STEP INTO LIVING THE VIBRATION OF THIS DREAM NOW?

Use this space to explore how you can step into *living the vibration* of this dream now.

SIGNS AND SYNCHRONICITIES

THESE INCLUDE:
SYMBOLS, ANGEL NUMBERS, SONGS,
CONVERSATIONS, CHANCE MEETINGS, ETC.

DATE	SIGNS & SYNCHRONICITIES

CELEBRATING YOUR MANIFESTATION!

HOW DID I RECEIVE MY MANIFESTATION?

DID MY MANIFESTATION SURPRISE ME AT ALL?

THANK YOU UNIVERSE!

i follow the path less unknown,
where my intuition guides me
to opportunities that glow;
i stand in awe-struck wonder
as the river beneath me flows
and i float downstream
to a place that no one knows.

MY DREAMS & DESIRES

/ /

TODAY I AM DREAMING OF:

Use the spaces below to draw, write and explore your dream!

What can I see in this dream?

What can I hear in this dream?

What can I smell in this dream?

What can I feel in this dream?

HOW WILL I FEEL ONCE I HAVE RECEIVED & ACHIEVED THIS DREAM?

HOW CAN I ALIGN AND ALLOW THIS DREAM?

IS THERE ANYTHING I NEED TO LET GO OF TO MAKE ROOM FOR THIS DREAM?

DO I CURRENTLY NEED TO TAKE ACTION OR WAIT FOR THE NEXT STEP TO SHOW ITSELF TO ME?

WHO DO I NEED TO BECOME TO RECEIVE THIS DREAM?

MY CHOSEN SONG FOR THIS DREAM:

----

*Listen to this song and visualise/feel the reality of your dreams coming true on a daily basis - then, let the Universe show you the next step!

PATHWAYS OF RECEIVING

LIST ALL THE WAYS THIS DREAM COULD HAPPEN:

HOW CAN I STEP INTO LIVING THE VIBRATION OF THIS DREAM NOW?

Use this space to explore how you can step into *living the vibration* of this dream now.

SIGNS AND SYNCHRONICITIES

THESE INCLUDE:
SYMBOLS, ANGEL NUMBERS, SONGS, CONVERSATIONS, CHANCE MEETINGS, ETC.

DATE	SIGNS & SYNCHRONICITIES

CELEBRATING YOUR MANIFESTATION!

HOW DID I RECEIVE MY MANIFESTATION?

DID MY MANIFESTATION SURPRISE ME AT ALL?

THANK YOU UNIVERSE!

every day, i wake up with a glow
and feel the love beneath
what is here and now
and as i appreciate
the smallest of things
my life becomes a blessing
birthed by angel wings.

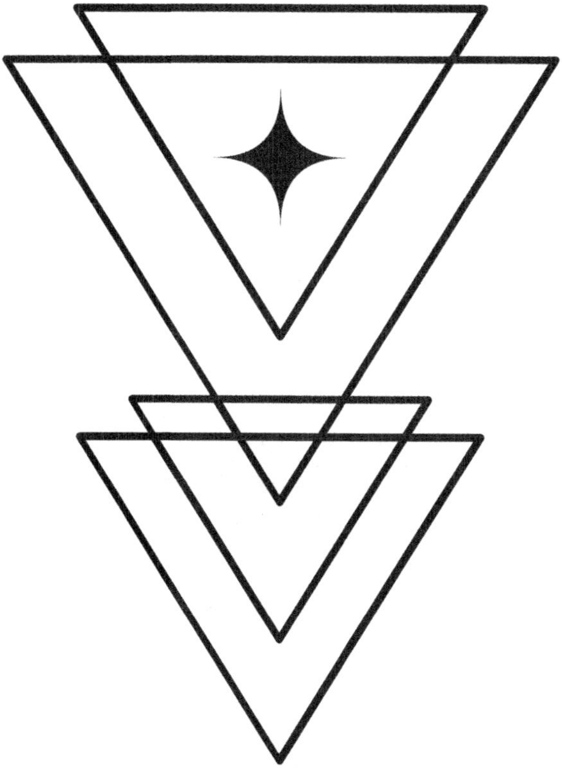

MY DREAMS & DESIRES

/ /

TODAY I AM DREAMING OF:

Use the spaces below to draw, write and explore your dream!

What can I see in this dream?

What can I hear in this dream?

What can I smell in this dream?

What can I feel in this dream?

HOW WILL I FEEL ONCE I HAVE RECEIVED & ACHIEVED THIS DREAM?

HOW CAN I ALIGN AND ALLOW THIS DREAM?

IS THERE ANYTHING I NEED TO LET GO OF TO MAKE ROOM FOR THIS DREAM?

DO I CURRENTLY NEED TO TAKE ACTION OR WAIT FOR THE NEXT STEP TO SHOW ITSELF TO ME?

WHO DO I NEED TO BECOME TO RECEIVE THIS DREAM?

MY CHOSEN SONG FOR THIS DREAM:

----

*Listen to this song and visualise/feel the reality of your dreams coming true on a daily basis - then, let the Universe show you the next step!

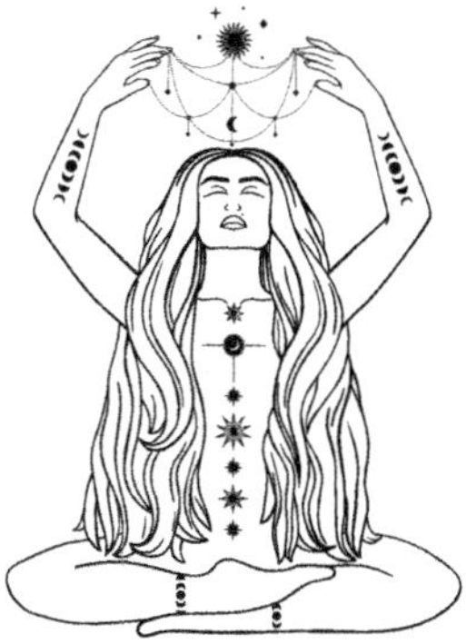

PATHWAYS OF RECEIVING

LIST ALL THE WAYS THIS DREAM COULD HAPPEN:

HOW CAN I STEP INTO LIVING THE VIBRATION OF THIS DREAM NOW?

Use this space to explore how you can step into *living the vibration* of this dream now.

SIGNS AND SYNCHRONICITIES

THESE INCLUDE:
SYMBOLS, ANGEL NUMBERS, SONGS, CONVERSATIONS, CHANCE MEETINGS, ETC.

DATE	SIGNS & SYNCHRONICITIES

CELEBRATING YOUR MANIFESTATION!

HOW DID I RECEIVE MY MANIFESTATION?

DID MY MANIFESTATION SURPRISE ME AT ALL?

THANK YOU UNIVERSE!

i call in guidance from near, far and wide
and pray that i follow **the path that is aligned**
for my soul's highest purpose,
my delight and joy;
so that i may shine bright
and live my full-blown life.

MY DREAMS & DESIRES

/ /

TODAY I AM DREAMING OF:

Use the spaces below to draw, write and explore your dream!

What can I see in this dream?

What can I hear in this dream?

What can I smell in this dream?

What can I feel in this dream?

HOW WILL I FEEL ONCE I HAVE RECEIVED & ACHIEVED THIS DREAM?

HOW CAN I ALIGN AND ALLOW THIS DREAM?

IS THERE ANYTHING I NEED TO LET GO OF TO MAKE ROOM FOR THIS DREAM?

DO I CURRENTLY NEED TO TAKE ACTION OR WAIT FOR THE NEXT STEP TO SHOW ITSELF TO ME?

WHO DO I NEED TO BECOME TO RECEIVE THIS DREAM?

MY CHOSEN SONG FOR THIS DREAM:

----

*Listen to this song and visualise/feel the reality of your dreams coming true on a daily basis - then, let the Universe show you the next step!

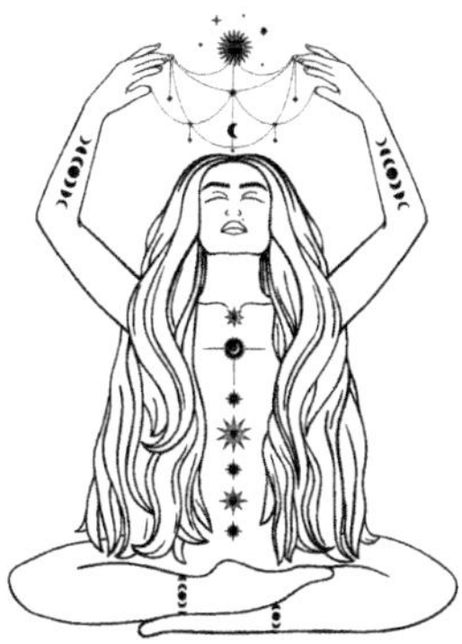

SIGNS AND SYNCHRONICITIES

THESE INCLUDE:
SYMBOLS, ANGEL NUMBERS, SONGS, CONVERSATIONS, CHANCE MEETINGS, ETC.

DATE	SIGNS & SYNCHRONICITIES

CELEBRATING YOUR MANIFESTATION!

HOW DID I RECEIVE MY MANIFESTATION?

DID MY MANIFESTATION SURPRISE ME AT ALL?

THANK YOU UNIVERSE!

as above, so below
and with **this knowledge**
i nurture, plant and sow
seeds from my heart
as i play the strings of the earth
and walk barefoot
into fields of gold.

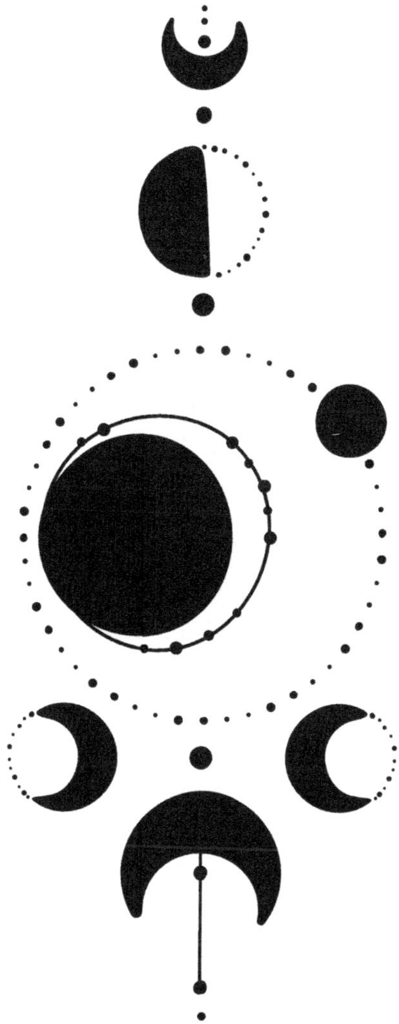

PATHWAYS OF RECEIVING

LIST ALL THE WAYS THIS DREAM COULD HAPPEN:

HOW CAN I STEP INTO LIVING THE VIBRATION OF THIS DREAM NOW?

Use this space to explore how you can step into *living the vibration* of this dream now.

SIGNS AND SYNCHRONICITIES

THESE INCLUDE:
SYMBOLS, ANGEL NUMBERS, SONGS, CONVERSATIONS, CHANCE MEETINGS, ETC.

DATE	SIGNS & SYNCHRONICITIES

CELEBRATING YOUR MANIFESTATION!

HOW DID I RECEIVE MY MANIFESTATION?

DID MY MANIFESTATION SURPRISE ME AT ALL?

THANK YOU UNIVERSE!

life isn't always simply **black and white**
sometimes grey clouds come
and shade my colourful life -
but when i feel heavy
and **don't know what to do**
i get down on my knees
and trust the only way out is through -
eventually, the clouds will fade and float away
and i will see my silver lining,
the birth of a brand-new day.

MY DREAMS & DESIRES

/ /

TODAY I AM DREAMING OF:

Use the spaces below to draw, write and explore your dream!

What can I see in this dream?

What can I hear in this dream?

What can I smell in this dream?

What can I feel in this dream?

HOW WILL I FEEL ONCE I HAVE RECEIVED & ACHIEVED THIS DREAM?

HOW CAN I ALIGN AND ALLOW THIS DREAM?

IS THERE ANYTHING I NEED TO LET GO OF TO MAKE ROOM FOR THIS DREAM?

DO I CURRENTLY NEED TO TAKE ACTION OR WAIT FOR THE NEXT STEP TO SHOW ITSELF TO ME?

WHO DO I NEED TO BECOME TO RECEIVE THIS DREAM?

MY CHOSEN SONG FOR THIS DREAM:

----

*Listen to this song and visualise/feel the reality of your dreams coming true on a daily basis - then, let the Universe show you the next step!

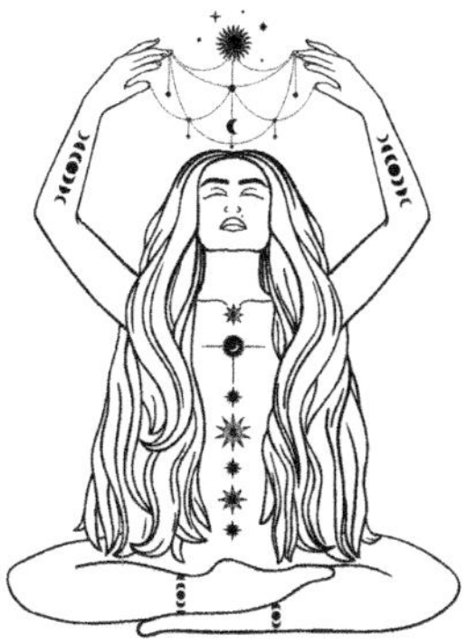

PATHWAYS OF RECEIVING

LIST ALL THE WAYS THIS DREAM COULD HAPPEN:

HOW CAN I STEP INTO LIVING THE VIBRATION OF THIS DREAM NOW?

Use this space to explore how you can step into *living the vibration* of this dream now.

SIGNS AND SYNCHRONICITIES

THESE INCLUDE:
SYMBOLS, ANGEL NUMBERS, SONGS, CONVERSATIONS, CHANCE MEETINGS, ETC.

DATE	SIGNS & SYNCHRONICITIES

CELEBRATING YOUR MANIFESTATION!

HOW DID I RECEIVE MY MANIFESTATION?

DID MY MANIFESTATION SURPRISE ME AT ALL?

THANK YOU UNIVERSE!

may i always be present
and **intrigued by the how**
whilst birthing my wildest dreams
from the powerful place of now.

MY DREAMS & DESIRES

/ /

TODAY I AM DREAMING OF:

Use the spaces below to draw, write and explore your dream!

What can I see in this dream?

What can I hear in this dream?

What can I smell in this dream?

What can I feel in this dream?

HOW WILL I FEEL ONCE I HAVE RECEIVED & ACHIEVED THIS DREAM?

HOW CAN I ALIGN AND ALLOW THIS DREAM?

IS THERE ANYTHING I NEED TO LET GO OF TO MAKE ROOM FOR THIS DREAM?

DO I CURRENTLY NEED TO TAKE ACTION OR WAIT FOR THE NEXT STEP TO SHOW ITSELF TO ME?

WHO DO I NEED TO BECOME TO RECEIVE THIS DREAM?

MY CHOSEN SONG FOR THIS DREAM:

----

*Listen to this song and visualise/feel the reality of your dreams coming true on a daily basis - then, let the Universe show you the next step!

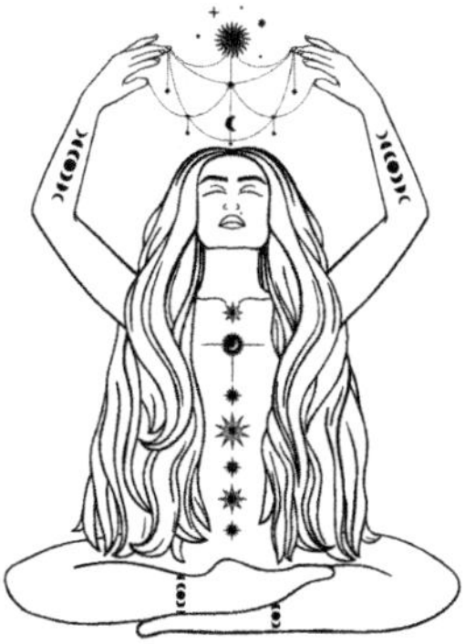

PATHWAYS OF RECEIVING

LIST ALL THE WAYS THIS DREAM COULD HAPPEN:

HOW CAN I STEP INTO LIVING THE VIBRATION OF THIS DREAM NOW?

Use this space to explore how you can step into *living the vibration* of this dream now.

SIGNS AND SYNCHRONICITIES

THESE INCLUDE:
SYMBOLS, ANGEL NUMBERS, SONGS, CONVERSATIONS, CHANCE MEETINGS, ETC.

DATE	SIGNS & SYNCHRONICITIES

CELEBRATING YOUR MANIFESTATION!

HOW DID I RECEIVE MY MANIFESTATION?

DID MY MANIFESTATION SURPRISE ME AT ALL?

THANK YOU UNIVERSE!

i didn't know how **powerful** i was
until i let my mindset shift -
and like the tide turning
waves of abundance poured in,
until one day i looked up
and **all that i could see**
were beautiful people and places,
waiting just for me.

MY DREAMS & DESIRES

/ /

TODAY I AM DREAMING OF:

Use the spaces below to draw, write and explore your dream!

What can I see in this dream?

What can I hear in this dream?

What can I smell in this dream?

What can I feel in this dream?

HOW WILL I FEEL ONCE I HAVE RECEIVED & ACHIEVED THIS DREAM?

HOW CAN I ALIGN AND ALLOW THIS DREAM?

IS THERE ANYTHING I NEED TO LET GO OF TO MAKE ROOM FOR THIS DREAM?

DO I CURRENTLY NEED TO TAKE ACTION OR WAIT FOR THE NEXT STEP TO SHOW ITSELF TO ME?

WHO DO I NEED TO BECOME TO RECEIVE THIS DREAM?

MY CHOSEN SONG FOR THIS DREAM:

----

*Listen to this song and visualise/feel the reality of your dreams coming true on a daily basis - then, let the Universe show you the next step!

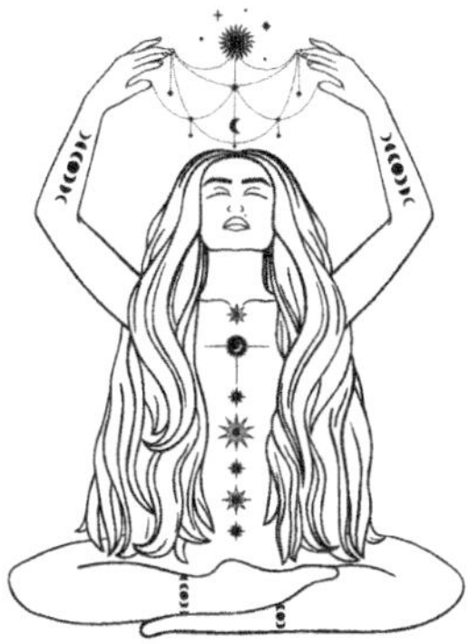

PATHWAYS OF RECEIVING

LIST ALL THE WAYS THIS DREAM COULD HAPPEN:

HOW CAN I STEP INTO LIVING THE VIBRATION OF THIS DREAM NOW?

Use this space to explore how you can step into *living the vibration* of this dream now.

SIGNS AND SYNCHRONICITIES

THESE INCLUDE:
SYMBOLS, ANGEL NUMBERS, SONGS, CONVERSATIONS, CHANCE MEETINGS, ETC.

DATE	SIGNS & SYNCHRONICITIES

CELEBRATING YOUR MANIFESTATION!

HOW DID I RECEIVE MY MANIFESTATION?

DID MY MANIFESTATION SURPRISE ME AT ALL?

THANK YOU UNIVERSE!

just when i think
i have everything i desire
a new dream lands in my head
and **my heart goes wild;**
i give thanks for the contrast
and everything **i have experienced in this life**
and smile at the fact
that life will always be -
one wild ride.

MY DREAMS & DESIRES

/ /

TODAY I AM DREAMING OF:

____

Use the spaces below to draw, write and explore your dream!

What can I see in this dream?

What can I hear in this dream?

What can I smell in this dream?

What can I feel in this dream?

HOW WILL I FEEL ONCE I HAVE RECEIVED & ACHIEVED THIS DREAM?

HOW CAN I ALIGN AND ALLOW THIS DREAM?

IS THERE ANYTHING I NEED TO LET GO OF TO MAKE ROOM FOR THIS DREAM?

DO I CURRENTLY NEED TO TAKE ACTION OR WAIT FOR THE NEXT STEP TO SHOW ITSELF TO ME?

WHO DO I NEED TO BECOME TO RECEIVE THIS DREAM?

MY CHOSEN SONG FOR THIS DREAM:

----

*Listen to this song and visualise/feel the reality of your dreams coming true on a daily basis - then, let the Universe show you the next step!

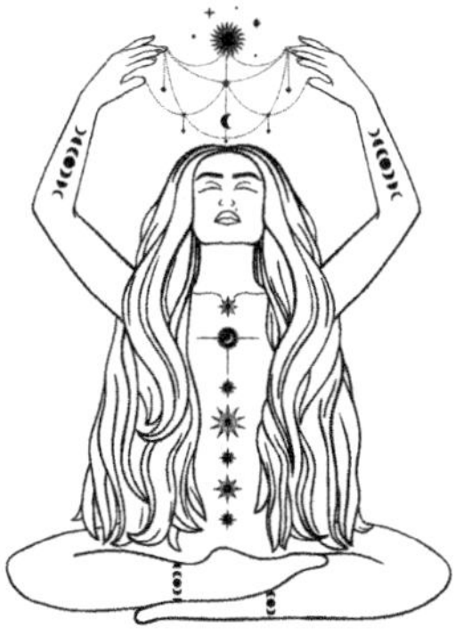

PATHWAYS OF RECEIVING

LIST ALL THE WAYS THIS DREAM COULD HAPPEN:

HOW CAN I STEP INTO LIVING THE VIBRATION OF THIS DREAM NOW?

Use this space to explore how you can step into *living the vibration* of this dream now.

SIGNS AND SYNCHRONICITIES

THESE INCLUDE:
SYMBOLS, ANGEL NUMBERS, SONGS, CONVERSATIONS, CHANCE MEETINGS, ETC.

DATE	SIGNS & SYNCHRONICITIES

CELEBRATING YOUR MANIFESTATION!

HOW DID I RECEIVE MY MANIFESTATION?

DID MY MANIFESTATION SURPRISE ME AT ALL?

THANK YOU UNIVERSE!

Printed in Great Britain
by Amazon

40384845R00069